The Path of Life

By

Bruce P. Burns, Ph.D.

Bloomington, IN  Milton Keynes, UK
authorHOUSE®

AuthorHouse™
1663 Liberty Drive, Suite 200
Bloomington, IN 47403
www.authorhouse.com
Phone: 1-800-839-8640

AuthorHouse™ UK Ltd.
500 Avebury Boulevard
Central Milton Keynes, MK9 2BE
www.authorhouse.co.uk
Phone: 08001974150

First published by AuthorHouse 4/18/2007

ISBN: 0-7596-4478-0

Printed in the United States of America
Bloomington, Indiana

This book is printed on acid-free paper.

Recommended reading

Survival of American Democracy
(Virtual Reality vs. Actual Reality, a Metaphor, and
the Irony of Christianity)

Abide in Him
(And Be Free)

The Man From The Fifth Dimension

ACKNOWLEDGMENTS

Appreciation to the work of my reader,

Rev. Henry F. "Jack" Brown, M. Div.

Who has been a Pastor, confessor, and friend for many years and who I admire and respect for his character, his open mind, and his rich background of reading.

DEDICATION

I dedicate this to that 'angel' who is my soul mate and has been with me, aiding me through this entire work.

"Thou wilt show me the path of life:
In Thy presence is fullness of joy;
At Thy right hand there are
Pleasures for evermore"

Psalm 16:11

TABLE OF CONTENTS

PART 1

PART 2

PART 3

PART 1

THE GREAT ASSUMPTION

To give this work its proper launching or christening one needs to ask himself; what ever happened to the awe and wonder that we humans should naturally have toward our Creator? One can wonder whether or not for the most part it has been dissipated by the marvelous achievements of human society? Do we after all worship man, in the final analysis?

Working with couples, families and individuals, as a clinical psychologist, for over thirty years, the question kept coming to mind. In doing psychotherapy in private practice to people in all walks of life, some of them at the top of their profession or career, why were so many people who appeared to have everything, so empty and lonely? What was the answer? Psychology alone couldn't fill in all the gaps in their lives.

All this leads me to the following assumption or premise, I will use the Bible as the main source of my present inquiry since it is held up as the Word of God. Assuming for the sake of argument that this is true, what better place to learn about God? Please keep in mind that your patience and tolerance is a prerequisite of this particular learning experience.

In the first chapter of Genesis God created the world and everything in it, including Man and Woman and He saw that everything was 'very good', not perfect but 'very good', this is an important distinction.

In the second chapter from the seventh verse the references are to Man 'formed' of the dust of the ground who became a 'living soul'. Later Woman is was 'made' from the rib of Man. (Who knows what period of time existed from Genesis 2:4 to Genesis 2:25?) Evil was already in the world, there are references to the tree of the knowledge of good and evil existing, and to Lucifer, Satan, the devil, and the serpent.

Let us assume that the first creation of Man and Woman were archetypes (ideal models) for the future perfected men and women and that some evil influence (say Satan) corrupted the archetypal humans. Perhaps that is indicated by the use of the words 'formed' and 'made'?* It may be a case of the 'very good' having to pass through suffering and overcome corruption to become perfect, for some reason not yet stated. There are many mysteries surrounding God and His dealings that we still do not understand. It is wise to keep in mind that we are merely creatures even if we may be God's greatest and highest 'handiwork'. It does appear from the Bible that it is in this area of pride that both

Man and Satan (Lucifer) fell. That is, thinking they were equal to or greater than God.

Back to the Book to determine the reason for suffering, and perhaps even to get a clue as to the part evil plays in the order of things. The New Testament reveals something not fully appreciated in the Old Testament, by the Jewish church leaders. This is often called the Gospel or good news. It states something not only new but good. There was and is a second creation in Christ: "...Except a man be born again, he cannot see the kingdom of God" (John 3:3b); "Therefore if any man be in Christ, he is a new creature: old things are passed away; behold, all things are become new." (2Corinthians 5:17); "And I saw a new heaven and a new earth: for the first heaven and the first earth were passed away; and there was no more sea." (Revelation 21:1).

Now what progress have we made? We have arrived at this stage with more questions than answers, perhaps more questions than we had before we started the book. We will probably get more questions before we get some answers but then often things get worse before they get better. God's 'very good' archetypal man may have had to suffer in order to be perfected and become incorruptible. "...If so be that we suffer with Him, that we may be also glorified together." (Romans 8:17b)

Satan (if he exists), sin, death and the 'self' all make us suffer, they all can corrupt the 'very good'. If Satan or the devil exists, it is logical to think that he would want us to discount, deny, caricature him, and mythicize him. This would give him a much freer hand as well as passing the buck to God. That is, if the devil does not exist, who can we blame for all the pain and suffering, other than ourselves? It is human nature to want to place the blame outside of ourselves especially when it is the 'self' who sins through greed and lust. Today most thinking people will admit there is evil in the world and it is most important we attribute it to the right cause. Satan is always the origin or basic source of it and often men add their own contributions. There appears to be a cosmic battle going on between good and evil, the human race seems to be a pawn caught in the middle.

It is many Christians' belief that through transcending love, evil will be conquered. Transcending love is the nature Jesus Christ displayed in dying for those who hated Him! Christians get involved through faith in God and obedience to Him. The only place one can learn about God and what He wants of us is in the Bible; there is no other source that deals so fully with Him and presents love as the answer. No other faith has a leader that is Divine and rose from the dead. The faith that this takes is a gift from Him and can be found only through Christ Jesus.

Without being judgmental or blaming let us try to examine some of the background and see if we can build a structure from what we read that will support these conclusions. There are so many places to start, so I will arbitrarily pick one, one which you might not have selected, but if the Bible is what Christians claim it is, we should eventually arrive at the same place. I chose the following study route because today there is so much criticism against the churches and many of their members. There is much apathy among many of the members themselves with the result of half empty churches. It is not uncommon to observe a skeptical attitude and a low opinion, among the populace, about those who call themselves Christians.

In Christ's revelation to John He spoke about 'lukewarm' Christians. "I know thy works, that thou art neither cold nor hot: I would thou wert cold or hot. So then because thou art lukewarm, and neither cold nor hot, I will spue thee out of My mouth." (Revelation 3:15-16) What do you think a lukewarm Christian is like? First it sounds like an oxymoron because my understanding of Christianity is that it foments (or is supposed to) a civil war within ones self, that is, it pits the desires of the flesh against the aspirations of the spirit. It also engages the adherent in a peaceful revolution against the things of the world, yet obeys authority and does not engage itself in the killing fields of politics and of religions. So it would be assumed that Christ was speaking of the same, 'lukewarm' group when He said, "This people draweth nigh unto me with their mouth, and honoureth Me with their lips; but their heart is far from me." (Matthew 15:8)

It is so hard not to fall into this group. Surprisingly enough, however, one does not have to be the center of admiration or of great works to fall into the other or 'hot' (dedicated) group. A follower can live a 'life hid with Christ in God', (Colossians 3:3) by being a regular citizen who lives a life of love, caring for others with a faith in Christ that blesses him or her with the fruits of the Spirit, such as: peace, love, joy, etc. Such a person may be a wife or mother or some common citizen whose life, charity and faith, go unnoticed by the world.

The so called 'cold' might be those who had consciously rejected Christianity, perhaps because of the hypocrisy of many of its followers or because of 'logical' thought on the matter; still another reason might be because of a tragedy, loss, or handicap. There might be more hope for such a one since there would be little danger of self-righteous smugness. That person would be more open to change and a new viewpoint. As he or she experiences growth through serious contemplation or exposure to a person or circumstance that makes him or her take notice and reassess his or her position.

In this age of the rapid progress of science and fast pace of life so many get left behind in one way or another and life becomes tedious. The search for diversion or entertainment becomes a consuming way of life to escape what Thoreau called, "...lives of quiet desperation."

Are we asking how life could be or what it is that we want? Are we asking more than how we can live a balanced life? Are we in reality looking for more than that, in the resolution of our quest concerning life?

*The Hebrew words for 'formed' man and 'made' man can indicate to 'squeeze' into a mold or 'shape' also to 'practice' or 'prepare'.

This could carry the implication of a process of perfecting, perhaps by pressure or trial and error, as a potter molds and shapes.

THE PRESENT SITUATION

The United States of America was established through force and violence. Yet it was from its beginning, by and large, a group of settlements espousing Christian beliefs. Thus it was involved in schism from its beginning, a double minded people, and it has continued to run this inconsistent course. Little wonder that so much confusion and contradiction are present in our politics, religion, and behavior.

Is not it time to realize that Christianity is an inward entity being outwardly expressed, independently of borders, politics, race and ethnicity? Thus Christians are truly not of this world even though actively in this world expressing love after the example of their master and savior, Jesus Christ. He was truly man in that He had righteous indignation, rarely expressed, and used force without hate and without physical harm to anyone (e.g., the fig tree and the money-changers in the temple, both described in Mark 11:12-21). He was also truly God: He performed miracles, presented the perfect solution to all of man's problems, and arose from the dead. He is alive today. He answers their prayers; gives them the Holy Spirit, Who enables them to follow God's commandments of love and Who

10

graces them with the Fruits of the Spirit (peace, love, joy, faith, etc.). Thus claims the Bible. Many Christians have experienced this.

We are born once, physically. We can be born a second time, spiritually and spend a lifetime overcoming sin and Satan's corruption, through Christ, which eventuates in sinless perfection and deathless life in God's perfect Kingdom, which is the second Creation.

Furthermore, Christianity forms the Church which is the body of Christ, He being the head. This Church is a living organism and exemplifies how it is that God is among us; our faith is one of interrelationships. Each is dependent upon the other. One is no more important than the other and all serve in their own assigned ways. We are in act and in fact becoming one with Christ and through this process we are increasingly in God as He is in us. We are to love all. We are not to be judgmental. No one knows who is, has been or will be chosen and thus become a member of the Kingdom of God and therefore be a part of the body of Christ and one with the rest of the Christians.

"After all, no one ever hated his own body, but he feeds and cares for it, just as Christ does the Church-for we are members of His body." (Ephesians 5:29-30). The claim is herewith made, **we live by faith because sensual experience is inadequate to explain**

existence. Only Christ can atone for our sins, nothing we can sacrifice can excuse our behavior before God. If we lie, cutting out our tongue will not achieve forgiveness. If we steal or rob, cutting off our arms will not secure forgiveness. If we commit adultery, mutilating our organs will not excuse it. There is no sacrifice we can make that will propitiate God.

In other words there is more to living than just being alive! As Christians we must be (become) locked into God and this connection is invisible and 'unthinkable' (that is, it is not achieved by thought but rather by faith-which is a gift and after this gift is given and received then thought often plays a part in the growth [or the 'becoming process']). The term being 'born again' is a birthing process and first we are conceived (receive faith); second we are in a period of gestation (working out what God works in), third comes our new birth. Then we are children of God and grow into adulthood becoming men and women of God. This conversion from the sensual to the spiritual is a process that varies in length of time with the individual. It is in this process that a creature of God has a part in his or her own creation. That is, he or she can choose to become an immortal spiritual creation or remain a created animal (perhaps damned to spend eternity in association with the devil and evil selves). The foregoing, as I read it, is what the Bible avers.

Thus, Christianity is a cosmic drama and a life long one at that. It is wrought out at the human level involving good and evil, God and Satan. There is no ultimate meaning for a human until he or she becomes and lives as a Christian, in fact a person is not a Christian unless he or she lives it. Let us be clear, many people live in a counterfeit 'faith', that is they claim to be Christians and espouse its principles but do not live them!

God loves us through other people and God loves other people through us. In other words we are all part of one body-Christ's, as members of His Church of which He is the Head. Faith is a gift from God without which experience is inadequate to explain existence. Suffering is a refiner's fire that purifies a Christian. Hurt and loss are a potter's kiln and wheel which in combination with Christ's salvation make Christians a new creation. We do not earn or deserve salvation, we accept it and suffer for it which is the true paradox of faith, being quite different from counterfeit 'faith'. Counterfeits are always close copies of the real thing. Ironically, Satan often serves God's purpose by bringing about conversion to Christ, through the suffering and tragedy Satan causes. The stronger one becomes in the Holy Spirit, the more joy and peace he has in the

Lord and the more he is able to love. **Christianity is a drama of life not a set of rules or rituals**. The Apostles revealed Christ to us and Christ revealed God to us Who gifted us with faith through His grace. We are all members of one body, the Church, whose head is Christ. God loves us and we will be His forever, "... being confident of this, that He Who began a good work in you will carry it on to completion until the day of Christ Jesus." (Philippians 1:6).

Before we talk about **The Church** itself, let us define it. First there is **The Church** which is the Body of Christ of which He is the head. It consists of all the true worshippers in all the various denomination, sects and divisions throughout Christendom. In other words, I may be a Methodist, Baptist, or Catholic, for example, but this does not make me a part of the Body of Christ, nor for that matter does it mean that I am in **The Church**. I am in **a** church, but that does not mean necessarily that I belong to **The Church** (that is, the Body of Christ). In fact, I may not belong to any brick and mortar church, but I may be a part of the Christian community. I may not be a Baptist, Methodist, Catholic, Pentecostal, Lutheran, Orthodox, or Episcopal, for example, and yet I may belong to **The Church**. The Lord said, 'Where two or more are gathered together, in My Name, I am there.' The operational phrase here is, 'in My Name'. What does that mean? Well, first of all it means by being in 'His Name' that we believe in Him. To believe in Him is to obey His commands and to understand and accept Who He is and why He is.

It may be that two, three, six, twelve, or any number may meet in different homes to read the Bible and pray, thereby attending a 'church'-which could be at least a part of The Church.

WHAT WENT WRONG?

It is not past time, it is never too late for us to sort out our priorities and values and straighten out our lives. The Christian claim is that no one can do this without the help of God, the Holy Spirit. This cannot be earned as no human deserves paradise. If we are given the gift of faith in Jesus Christ and live it, then we will eventually enter Paradise. Sometimes one knows that much from early Sunday School training, which is often later rejected as a young person. If that has been the case then we need to determine to read the Bible carefully, starting with the New Testament and then proceeding to the Old Testament and to begin trying to pray. Many of us know without too much thought that we can be arrogant and unfeeling. It is not that one does not love anybody or that he does not do good things or lead a 'good' life. But somewhere inside there may be the gnawing fear that he has been too casual about what life means and whether there is any real and abiding purpose to life.

So what follows are reflections and conclusions resulting from a long study of the Bible and a review of life's mistakes and lessons. So much depends upon what (or rather Who) one believes in as well as what it actually means to 'believe'. The Bible states that being part of the Church* is necessary and sufficient for one to enter eternal life in Paradise. However, it must be said that the mouth craves what the stomach rejects, when it comes to the battle between the flesh and the spirit.

Israel failed God as they were to be a nation of priests, bringing the true God to the rest of the world. Instead they kept Him to themselves, in a very exclusive manner. Instead of being spiritual they became increasingly proud. Likewise today many churches are, by and large, failing the nations of the world and themselves. Many church members have become either very materialistic or exclusionary instead of becoming spiritual and reaching out. They have become judgmental instead of loving. Post-Apostolic Doctrines and man-made dogmas (I call both 'theological') can get in the way of principles. More on this later.

One can read the Gospel of John for a primer on love or the Letters of Paul for selflessness. Paul's letter to the Romans is a classic and the most profound statement of Christianity we have. Even so the message of Christ is simplicity itself, and although it is straightforward it is impossible even for the 'born again' to achieve perfection. (That will come in the next life, when Christ gives us our glorified bodies).

It is getting a little 'heavy', is it not? But please keep reading, it is not as bad as it sounds. In order to follow the teachings of Jesus Christ we must acknowledge that we are sinners and that we need the help of the Holy Spirit to walk after Christ, to know Him. Thus to 'believe' in Him is not like that of the devils, who 'believe and tremble'; we must love and live our belief. When our life is over we do not want to hear, "Depart from Me, I never knew you! This people draweth nigh unto Me with their mouth and honoureth Me with their lips; but their heart is far from Me."(Matthew 15:8). It is necessary to be part of His Church but not sufficient merely to go to a church.

As most of us know Jesus Christ is the only Holy begotten Son of God. Men put Him to death because all men are born into evil and cannot by their own efforts extricate themselves from evil, no matter how 'good' they try to be. We are 'born again' of the Spirit through His blood which was sacrificed for us even though we do not love God naturally. This was God's grace and reveals the type of love called 'agape' which is His gift to us, undeserved, unmerited and cannot be earned. Through His blood we are 'begotten' also but as adopted sons and daughters of God. Thus we are born by water (natural birth), redeemed by accepting

Christ's blood (Christ's sacrifice) and begotten of the Spirit (living after the spirit rather than the flesh).

Thus we must: 1)accept Christ; 2)worship God with other Christians; 3)study the Bible and put it into practice; 4)walk after the Spirit (this includes renouncing sin and witnessing for Christ); 5)pray. As all of us who have tried, have found out that these can be done only through the Holy Spirit helping and teaching our spirit. The Lord said, "The Spirit itself beareth witness with our spirit, that we are the children of God." (Romans 8:16). He also said, "God is a Spirit: and they that worship Him must worship Him in spirit and in truth." (John 4:24). We are not only mind and body, which are mortal; but we are also spirit, which is eternal.

My personal belief is that only the rational thinking human has spirit which changes once we accept Christ and allow the Holy Spirit to convert our spirit. This is reflected by our soul. The Spirit essentially develops our spirit. One example: Paul said, "For though I be absent in the flesh, yet am I with you in the spirit, joying and beholding your order and the steadfastness of your faith in Christ..." (Colossians 2:5). If you take this in the context of all the letters of Paul it can be seen that he meant this literally. There are many more dramatic abilities of the Human spirit when it becomes one with the Holy Spirit, as many of the Apostles displayed, raising the dead, healing, etc.

Before we go further it seems appropriate to pursue the question, why are so many churches either lifeless or practically empty today? Is it because God insists on our putting faith into practice? For some reason, God places great importance upon having faith in Him. "But without faith it is impossible to please Him: for he that cometh to God must believe that He is, and that He is a rewarder of them that diligently seek Him." (Hebrews 11:6). I think the importance of faith is related to why evil exists, which is a mystery, and I won't attempt to tie it in at this point.

Setting aside Satan's involvement for the moment. There are two powerful cultural forces at work that contribute to the decline of the churches.

1) Stop and think how the media (all forms of media) attempt to scoff at faith in God. This runs all the way from labeling all Christians as the 'Christian Right' and as extremists, inferring that they are all fanatics, if they in any way are Bible believing; to declaring that Christianity is only for the weak and the losers. Furthermore they tout science as the answer to everything. This is done to the point that it seems like some sinister collusion, a devilish conspiracy. Let us take a little more time and examine two such cases.

Take the 'Theory of Evolution', which is indeed a theory of which part is unsubstantiated by facts! In Darwin's second book, "The Descent of Man and Selection in Relation to Sex" (1871), in chapter 21 his second sentence opens with: "Many of the views which have been advanced are highly speculative, and some no doubt will prove erroneous;..." Then in the last sentence he states: "False facts are highly injurious to the progress of science, for they often endure long but false views if supported by some evidence, do little harm,..."

In his second paragraph he is guilty of what he had just finished advising, as above, to wit; "...The main conclusion here arrived at, and now held by many naturalists who are well competent to form a sound judgment is that man is descended from some less highly organized form. The grounds upon which this conclusion rests will never be shaken,..." Here he puts forth a view which he then states as an unshakable fact and it is all based on the observation that because there are similar organs or vestiges of them in two different organisms, therefore one descended from the other, this is a non-sequitor (does not follow), it is a speculation which is unscientific but is defended vigorously as a fact!

What Darwin does is to make factual observations and then jumps to the conclusion that these prove a relationship exists and states what that relationship is, both of which are surmises and yet he goes on to say that they, "...are facts which cannot be disputed." He further states that anyone who does not accept these 'conclusions' as facts instead of as surmises, is looking at the phenomena of nature-"like a savage"...

There are few examples in the history of science where more credulous things have been accepted as fact as they have been in 'thorough-going' evolution. 'Thorough-going' evolution is based upon surmise and conjecture in its attempt to 'disprove', "...that man is the work of a separate act of creation." Evolution has been helpful and illuminating except when you get to the foregoing extreme type of 'thorough-going' evolution which assumes the connection of man to lower forms of life because of similarity of organs or vestiges of body parts. It rejects the notion of a supreme Creator Who created Man as a separate and unique entity.

Another case in point is Freudian Psychology, although it has had many illuminating insights into the workings of the mind and human relationships. However in its extreme form it goes too far as well, stating there is no God, only 'Eros', (instinct). Freud cleverly replaced the animal nature of man with the 'id', and substituted the self with the 'ego', and the spirit with the 'super ego'. He replaced Satan with 'Thanatos', the death instinct.

2.)The other great cultural force opposing Christian faith is peer pressure. Consider this, especially today with our central schools, television, the breakdown of what is right and what is wrong, based on the absolutes of the Ten Commandments. Today in secular society everything is relative. Often the rule is, if it feels good do it. The peer pressure on children is extreme to conform and this has spread to teenagers and adults. If you stick up for principles of right and wrong or strength of character or a Christian life style, you are branded as weird or almost forced into being solitary. All of this fosters doubt about God's importance, existence and interest in us. Finally, we must admit that the way Christendom has split up into sects and denominations and divisions, coupled with so much wrangling and disputes caused by different, man-made doctrines and dogmas, has had much to do with this. The hypocrisy on the part of many church goers, doesn't help.

If we are Christians we must not be prisoners of our six senses: visual, auditory, olfactory, gustatory, tactile and proprioceptive (inner body sensation and bio-feedback). <u>That is, we are not to **cater** to them so that they **dominate** or control our thoughts or behavior.</u>

If this happens we become prisoners of our body. If we are not controlled by our senses, then no matter what happens to us physically or psychologically it has minimal control over our emotions or our spirit. "If the Son therefore shall make you free, ye shall be free indeed." (John 8:36). This is the ultimate cure for addictions, phobias, compulsions, obsessions, anxiety, depression and paranoia. The forgoing requirements are clear enough to agree with them, but does that make one a Christian? If so, in what way does it change ones life? How would a person behave and think differently if he were not a Christian?

This raises several serious issues. For example, does acknowledging that one is a Christian mean that he admits to being a sinner? This entails understanding what is meant by sin, and doing something about it namely repenting which means not only being sorry and remorseful but trying to stop sinning. Yes! There is still hope that God can deliver us, despite these Satanic and cultural forces and harmful human influences.

*Keep in mind that belonging to The Church (capitalized) is to believe Jesus Christ is the resurrected, divine Son of God. Calling (in prayer) on the Holy Ghost is essential to living in obedience to Christ. Attending a Catholic or Protestant church, is not enough.

GETTING IT STRAIGHT

The point most of us arrive at, if we have been actively and sincerely trying to stop sinning, is that we cannot do it alone. This brings up the definition of sin, what is sin? It is selfishness, self-centeredness, lusting (even if it is only in the mind), greed, hurting others, active homosexuality, promiscuity, etc. The list can be lengthened with further reading of the Bible. We find, in fact, that the New Testament is even more inclusive than the Ten Commandments and extends even to the intent or desire, over and beyond the actual deed. Now, with such a difficult task as this we most assuredly need to able to call upon God for help and receive some kind of encouragement.

We do receive confirmation and begin to sense change and growth! As we grow in this spiritual life we find our old nature (sinful) is losing control over us and God rewards us. We are more aware of the fruits of the Spirit such as: love, joy, peace, patience, gentleness, goodness, faith, moderation and humility, increasing in our lives. They are also becoming progressively more important to us and valued by us-over and above the old sensual pleasures that revolved around our self and involved our six physical senses. (The sixth sense is called proprioceptive and means the internal biofeed-back of being in a physical state of pleasure such as might be arrived at through alcohol, drugs, an ego trip, sex, or some other kind of false homeostasis[that is equilibrium] attained physiologically or psychologically.) These are counterfeits of the joy of true peace and love given by the Holy Spirit. This is not to say that marital love-making is a sin, just that sexual intercourse (outside of a loving marriage) is not love-making it is using a person as an object and brings about greater loneliness and emptiness.

Because of the difficulty of this struggle and the prevalence of evil in the world, we are brought face to face with the problem of evil. Why does it exist especially since we believe in a good and loving Creator? Evil must exist for a purpose and as one carefully surveys this problem one is led inevitably to the thought that we are here precisely to deal with evil and to glorify God in so doing. According to the Bible, love is the antidote to evil. But evil will not be fully overcome until God comes back again on our earthly plane. He was here once in the form of Jesus Christ, the fullness of the Godhead bodily. In sacrificing His Son He, in effect, Himself died on the cross, for us. What greater love could He have exhibited for us?! The foregoing involves the mystery of the Trinity. To reside eternally in His paradise, rests upon dependency on the Cross and the Blood of Jesus Christ and walking after the Spirit. There could be no greater hell than to spend eternity without God and with the potentially unlimited badness of even good <u>human animals</u>.

So what does God expect (demand) of us? That we live lives hid with Christ in God. As Micah said in the Old Testament in chapter 6 verse 8: "He hath showed thee, O man, what is good; and what doth the LORD require of thee, but to do justly, and to love mercy, and to walk humbly with thy God?" Metaphorically speaking I am in a boat(Christ) on the ocean(God) and no matter what the storms, I sail, keep afloat and hold my course with the aid of my rudder(Holy Spirit). In Paradise there will be no knowledge of good and evil because evil will not exist, we will eat only of the fruit of the tree of life and enter into a timeless and ecstatic paradise of love, peace and joy that we never dreamt could exist.

Christ is the blood sacrifice which washes away the believer's sin, once and for all the Christian is exonerated from his sins; Christ is his atonement. Christ is the sacrifice, God makes the sacrifice and the believer is the recipient. The believers and not men in general are the recipients; it is through God's gift of faith that men become believers in Jesus. They cannot earn this gift; it is predestined before birth and it is both the necessary and the sufficient grounds for salvation. Are either salvation or security eternal? Who or what determines which men are gifted with faith and so are believers? The answer is, God and God alone; one man cannot judge another. Appearances will not decide the issue, it has already been decided-before the foundation of the world. Can an individual know whether or not he has faith and thus is destined for eternal life in God's paradise?

One answer is that he can have hope and that hope is given substance to the extent to which the feelings of the heart, thoughts of the mind and behavior of the body, are controlled by Christian love. Although self-deceit is possible, the Holy Spirit gives assurance to our spirit through His loving guidance and encouragement. It is a process that one can grow toward with more and more maturity. Although one can no more be 'half-saved' than 'half-pregnant', there are stages of growth in the sense of being merely 'half-alive' as compared to being 'fully-alive'.

When do I become a new creature in Christ? Can there be awareness of the Holy Spirit's presence? When do I receive a new heart? How is it brought about? If I have a new heart and am a 'new creature' in Christ, why do I keep on sinning? Why does my old nature keep hanging around and what does that mean? Does anything depend upon my conscious efforts and if so what? Is Christ alone necessary and sufficient for my salvation? In what way does Christ in me, change me? Can I lose my salvation? Does God deal with humans as individuals or as nations, races, or tribes? What is the problem 'goodness' can introduce, and what is 'hibernating' sin?

These issues and more are in the Bible. They will be approached in Part 2. Please keep in mind that the basic message is in Part 1. Part 2 is intended more for the student who is inquisitive and wants more answers. It will attempt to explore some of the more complex questions (unnecessary for either salvation or living a Christian life). It can be a snare and a pitfall for the type of intellectual that has to dot every i and cross every t, and wrap Christianity up in a neat little box with a ribbon tied around it. This is because it can lead to endless wrangling. After all, we are creatures and no matter how hard we try with our human logic, we will never be able to fully fathom our Creator, Almighty God, and solve all of life's mysteries.

One **can** find the central message of the Bible by putting into practice what one reads in it, day by day. There is no necessity of making it unnecessarily difficult. It is a matter of growing with other Christians, along with seeking the Holy Spirit's guidance.

PART 2

REFINING THE DETAILS

When you buy a Bible, it is helpful to get a red letter New Testament; this is one in which the words of God or Christ are in red. It is easier if you can get together with family and/or some friends to study it, read it, digest it, discuss it. It is best to begin with the New Testament. John really focuses on love whereas Paul is the great scholar of the New Testament. It is important not to allow previous training or hearsay to influence you so that you can read with an open mind. You owe this to yourself and your children; there is no study more important. It will equip you for life, comfort you and give purpose and meaning to your life. Try not to allow different interpretations to produce arguments and angry disagreement within the group.

Disagreement is okay, some of us may interpret passages differently-so what?! If we are sincere and trying to put our learning into practice and seek the help of the Holy Spirit through individual and group prayer, we will be guided and differences should be discussed and considered, but arguing about them is usually counterproductive. It is best not to try to convert others to one way of interpretation. Do discuss differences in a reasonable manner-do not argue or be contentious. In the final analysis it is between one's self and God, and if one's life reveals love and other fruits of the Spirit more and more, one is on the right track. Remember we do not have to convert the world or even our neighbors, they will come to us if our lifestyle is spiritual in a loving way. If our life and responses set another person on his quest for God and meaning for his life, we are not to get upset if he responds with a different interpretation. If he is sincere and we are maturing as Christians, we are to accept him and pray for him; he may in fact help us to grow more.

The answers to all questions mentioned in Part 1 can be found in the Bible. Some 'theological' doctrines can be helpful by putting into words which can draw a whole concept together and make some of the mysteries easier to grasp. But more often than not they set up divisions within Christendom and are probably more responsible for the disgraceful state of Christianity today than any other single factor. They separate people into factions; they set up opposing points of view creating denominations and major divisions that war with each other, judge each other, reject each other and in general have Christians rejecting, fighting and judging each other. This is the antithesis of what Christ preached.

Jesus' message is simple, straightforward, unifying and one of love to all and among all. Granted, although it is a simple message, it is not one easy to live. But the very difficulty (really impossibility) of living each of His commands, brings us to our knees seeking His help and admitting that we (all) are sinners. Some other 'theological' doctrines do, however, often serve a questionable purpose, and that is they sell books, and establish opposing theological seminaries. In the process they make some bookstores profitable, some seminaries counter-productive and some 'false churches' profitable. So even in matters of faith, commercialism intrudes and converts faith into religion.

Today there are at least three major sources of hindrance to finding (or even wanting to find) God. They are <u>sensualism, materialism and idolatry</u>.

<u>Sensualism</u> enslaves us to our bodies-namely our senses. That is, pleasing our taste, touch, hearing, seeing, smelling or that inner feedback from our body (proprioceptive or bio-feedback). This may result in obesity, pornographic preoccupation, excessive concentration on sounds (not all of which are music), creature comfort as a primary goal, addictions and other self-consuming physical excesses draining our energies.

Materialism focuses upon seeking power, control, money, acquisitions, or security, and any other insatiable lust for man-made or man-conceived creations.

Idolatry consists of hero worship, usually of sports figures, actors, rock stars, political, scientific leaders, or business tycoons. They are given magical qualities, to the extent of believing that merely touching or seeing them will somehow transfer some of the 'magic' to oneself. Lastly, the most prevalent form is unrecognized idolatry, which in our capitalistic society is the worship of money.

Faith needs to surpass thought and feeling; love is to supplant self; so that while one is functioning in the world-one is not **of** the world. This produces a life that is acceptable to the Lord and is a goal toward which one proceeds. It is a progressive process. Having more than one Bible translation can be helpful, e.g.; The King James Version and The New International Version, are two very good translations. The Biblical quotations used in this book are all from the King James Version unless otherwise specified. Success takes time and perseverance.

What does God require of us so that He will give us eternal life in His paradise?

1) Believing in Jesus Christ and His Way as the only road to salvation;
   a) Faith in Him as the only good, loving Creator,
   b) Trying to fulfill God's requirements concerning the way we live and think.

We must understand and accept that without faith in Him it is impossible to please God. Furthermore we cannot earn nor deserve His forgiveness nor acceptance. Our faith in Jesus Christ is a gift from God. This is shown, established and 'proven' by our 'walk', that is, how we think, feel and act. It is important to be clear on this last point, our 'walk' (some call it 'works') is merely a necessary but not sufficient passport to paradise. Faith in the goodness of God, and the bowing down to Jesus Christ as the Son of God, our Lord and Savior, is absolutely indispensable. But this is a gift. The presence of this gift is revealed only through our lives. This is what God alludes to as 'seeking Him', or abiding in Him.

So the question becomes how do we evidence our faith through our life? Following in the next part is a list of Biblical scriptures that could be helpful guideposts. This is not intended to be an exhaustive listing but could be heuristic, i.e., give insight. It must be added that the meaning of each passage of scripture is to be interpreted by each person, with the help of the Holy Ghost within, in other words it is between each individual and God. Two other factors enter in: 1) as one becomes more and better acquainted with the Bible the interpretations of some scriptures will change because we are maturing; and 2) individual passages need to be interpreted in the light of other passages. Finally it is so important to understand that this is a process and one in which a person will not only make progress but also one in which he will have set backs or backsliding as well as failures. We are not perfect, we are only striving for perfection while at the same time remaining and <u>functioning in this world</u>. Ones life is to be loving and seeking the fellowship of other Christians. We are not to be overcome by it all, nor by failures and doubt. One of the three cardinal requirements is hope (the other two are faith and love). Hope would not be necessary were it not for doubt. So doubt is a hindrance.

One of Satan's main weapons against us is creating doubt and breaking down our faith. The world joins him in this, especially through the media who tend to distort, deny and/or modify God's existence, message, and goodness. They also in one way or another may deny the existence of Satan, the extent of his evil and the identity of his followers.

The existence of evil, pain and suffering, make it all the harder to have faith. This, it seems to me, ties in with the importance of having and maintaining faith in God, His goodness and His caring. That is, faith and trust in God, at all times, in all ways, seems to be one of the most important goals that God demands of Christians. Problems, pain, and suffering all tend to either strengthen our faith or weaken it. But this is the one 'mine field' which we must cross. Paradoxically, we cannot do this without His help! The following is in one of Paul's letters to the Corinthians wherein he made a request to overcome a physical problem and the Lord said 'no' to him. In the following quotation, Paul tells us about the Lord's reply and Paul's response to it. "And He said unto me, My grace is sufficient for thee: for My strength is made perfect in weakness. Most gladly therefore will I rather glory in my infirmities, that the power of Christ may rest upon me." (2 Corinthians 12:9).

SEEKING AND FINDING

It is most important to assume (take on faith) that there is one basic truth to life, **GOD IS LOVE**. If you keep this maxim in mind while studying the Bible it will tend to guide you safely through the shoals of dogma, post-apostolic doctrine, schisms, sects, divisions and denominations. Also, as previously stated, it is wise to interpret individual passages in the light of others as well as in its particular context. Having said this let us continue on this vital pathway to life and its purposes, meanings and mysteries.

After looking at the passages of scripture in the next part, you may want to pick out a few that have meaning at this point in life, applying them to living as much as possible and gradually adding more and more scriptures as they become more personally meaningful. Going over them with trusted friends and other Christians often enlarges ones understanding (include Pastors and other clerics). We seek God's help through prayer, it is good to remember that God, Jesus Christ, and the Holy Spirit are all manifestations of God and in essence are One. The Holy Spirit, especially, will help interpret scripture. Prayer, discussion and studying the Bible are the a,b,c's for changing ones life and creating a living, vital faith which will result in a life that to an increasing degree is expressing: love, joy, peace, patience, gentleness, goodness, faith, moderation, and humility.

We will not understand all mysteries while we are in this life, no matter how much men explore, invent, study, experiment, or speculate. When we push too hard in matters of faith we can overreach our experience to such a degree that we may begin to distort or unnecessarily complicate our faith, even sometimes seemingly losing our faith in the process, for varying lengths of time. Our faith is simple and straightforward and as we put it into practice, it becomes strengthened and expands as our wisdom grows. From time to time it is good to read one or more of the following passages. It is rewarding after reading one of them to look it up in the Bible and read some of the scripture before and after the passage. Doing that helps to read with more concentration, interest and understanding than just by reading chapters of the Bible consecutively. There are times to read chapter by chapter while studying and learning the Bible. As the Bible states in 2 Timothy 2:15, "Study to shew thyself approved unto God, a workman that needeth not to be ashamed, rightly dividing the Word of Truth."

PASSAGES TO PARADISE

Here then are good passages to start out with, over time adding more and perhaps even replacing some. God speaks to us individually, utilizing the Holy Spirit, so that in the final analysis we should arrive at the same understanding as other Christians. But here again we are not to be contentious.

1.　When it seems everything in life tends to make us doubt, it is helpful to repeat the following, to remind us of how important our faith is to God, and to realize how much Satan is trying to make us doubt:

But without faith it is impossible to please Him: for he that cometh to God must believe that He is, and that He is a rewarder of them that diligently seek Him.

Hebrews 11:6

Now the God of hope fill you with all joy and peace in believing, that ye may abound in hope, through the power of the Holy Ghost.

Romans 15:13

For by grace are ye saved through faith; and that not of yourselves: it is the gift of God: Not of works, lest any man should boast. For we are his workmanship created in Christ Jesus unto good works which God hath before ordained that we should walk in them.

Ephesians 2:8-10

I can do all things through Christ which stengtheneth me.

Philippians 4:13

And we know that all things work together for good to them that love God, to them who are the called according to His purpose.

Romans 8:28

And God is able to make all grace abound toward you; that ye, always having all sufficiency in all things, may abound to every good work:

2 Corinthians 9:8

And hope maketh not ashamed; because the love of God is shed abroad in our hearts by the Holy Ghost which is given unto us.

Romans 5:5

2. When God seems far away the following verses will help to make Him more of a presence.

Jesus said unto him, Thou shalt love the Lord thy God with all thy heart, and with all thy soul, and with all thy mind.

This is the first and great commandment.

And the second is like unto it, Thou shalt love thy neighbor as thyself.

On these two commandments hang all the law and the prophets.

Matthew 22: 37-40

Not by might nor by power, but by My Spirit, says the Lord Almighty.

Zechariah 4:6b

Peace I leave with you, My peace I give unto you; not as the world giveth, give I unto you. Let not your heart be troubled, neither let it be afraid.

John 14:27

Be still, and know that I am God.

Psalm 46:10a

3. When one becomes fearful or anxious, the following is so comforting to repeat over and over, remembering, God is love! And He is with us, closer than our shadow, closer than our skin.

There is no fear in love, but perfect love casteth out fear: because fear hath torment. He that feareth is not made perfect in love.

1John 4:18

In God I have put my trust; I will not be afraid what man can do unto me.

Psalm 56:11

Herein is love, not that we loved God, but that He loved us, and sent His Son to be the propitiation for our sins.

1John 4:10

4. When we need to be reminded that even though His grace is such that He gives us all things freely, including faith-yet, He commands us to be fruitful, good neighbors, and good Samaritans.

But wilt thou know, O vain man, that faith without works is dead?

James 2:20

Even so faith, if it hath not works, is dead, being alone. Yea, a man may say, Thou hast faith, and I have works: shew me thy faith without works, and I will shew thee my faith by my works.

James 2:17-18

5. As you study the Bible, keep the following in mind, and when you pray ask for His truth. Reassure yourself with this verse.

And ye shall know the truth, and the truth shall make you free.

John 8:32

6. Keep the following in mind, especially when someone is trying your patience, also when you need to put things back into proportion.

And now abideth faith, hope, charity, these three, but the greatest of these is charity(love).

1Corinthians 13:13

Rejoice in the Lord always: and again I say, Rejoice. Let your moderation be known unto all men. The Lord is at hand. Be careful for nothing; but in everything by prayer and supplication with thanksgiving let your requests be made known unto God. And the peace of God, which passeth all understanding, shall keep your hearts and minds through Christ Jesus. Finally, brethren, whatsoever things are true, whatsoever things are honest, whatsoever things are just, whatsoever things are pure, whatsoever things are lovely, whatsoever things are of good report; if there be any virtue, and if there be any praise, think on these things.

Philippians 4:4-8

7. Sometimes we need a reminder that even though God is love and grace, we still need to follow Jesus' way and life and He needs to be a vital, ongoing model in our life.

Abide in Me, and I in you. As the branch cannot bear fruit of itself, except it abide in the vine; no more can ye, except ye abide in Me.

John 15:4

8.   Here again, the following verses of scripture that are so comforting, strengthening, and helpful, when we are having self doubts or are fearful. Especially when we go to bed at night if we meditate, to the degree of memorizing, the specific verses that fit our need.

For God hath not given us the spirit of fear; but of power, and of love, and of a sound mind.

2Timothy 1:7

Being confident of this very thing, that He which hath begun a good work in you will perform it until the day of Jesus Christ:

Philippians 1: 6

The Lord shall preserve thee from all evil: He shall preserve thy soul. The Lord shall preserve thy going out and thy coming in from this time forth, and even forevermore.

Psalm 121:7-8

9.   When it seems that we cannot do or complete what is set in front of us, cannot meet some challenge, bring Him into your life by repeating the following.

For it is God which worketh in you both to will and to do of His good pleasure.

Philippians 2:13

Wait on the Lord: be of good courage, and He shall strengthen thine heart: Wait, I say, on the Lord.

Psalm 27:14

You will keep in perfect peace him whose mind is stedfast, because he trusts in You.

Isaiah 26:3(NIV)

10. We will feel the drawing closeness of the Holy Spirit if we try to live in accordance with the following verses.

Jesus saith unto him, I am the way, the truth, and the life: no man cometh unto the Father, but by Me.

John 14: 6

...In repentance and rest is your salvation, in quietness and trust is your strength,...

Isaiah 30:15b

11. When we feel lost or helpless, these verses are such stabilizers and help us to go on.

We are saved by hope: but hope that is seen is not hope: for what a man seeth, why doth he yet hope for?

Romans 8:24

He will have no fear of bad news; his heart is steadfast, trusting in the lord. His heart is secure, he will have no fear; in the end he will look in triumph on his foes.

Psalm 112:7-8(NIV)

Take therefore no thought for the morrow: for the morrow shall take thought for the things of itself. Sufficent unto the day is the evil thereof.

Matthew 6:34

12. When we are fighting temptation and the odds seem overwhelming, call upon God with these scriptures.

Submit yourselves therefore to God. Resist the devil and he will flee from you.

James 4:7

There hath no temptation taken you but such as is common to man: but God is faithful, Who will not suffer you to be tempted above that ye are able; but will with the temptation also make a way to escape, that ye may be able to bear it.

1 Corinthians 10:13

And He said unto me, My grace is sufficient for thee: for My strength is made perfect in weakness. Most gladly therefore will I rather glory in my infirmities, that the power of Christ may rest upon me.

2 Corinthians 12:9

That they should seek the Lord, if haply they might feel after Him, and find Him, though He be not far from any one of us: For in Him we live, and move, and have our being;

Acts17:27-28a

Draw nigh to God, and He will draw nigh to you.

James 4: 8a

The Bible as beautiful literature.

In the beginning was the Word, and the Word was with God, and the Word was God. The same was in the beginning with God. All things were made

by Him; and without Him was not any thing made.
In Him was life; and the life was the light of men.
And the light shineth in darkness; and the darkness
comprehended it not.

John 1:1-5

In the beginning God created the heaven and the
earth. And the earth was without form, and void;
and darkness was upon the face of the deep. And
the Spirit of God moved upon the waters. And God
said, let there be light: and there was light. And God
saw the light, that it was good: and God divided the
light from the darkness. And God called the light
Day, and the darkness He called Night. And the
evening and the morning were the first day.

Genesis 1:1-5

The Lord is my shepard; I shall not want. He
maketh me to lie down in green pastures: He leadeth
me beside the still waters. He restoreth my soul:
He leadeth me in the paths of righteousness for His
name's sake. Yea, though I walk through the valley
of the shadow of death, I will fear no evil: for Thou
art with me; Thy rod and Thy staff they comfort me.
Thou preparest a table before me in the presence of
mine enemies: Thou anointest my head with oil; my

cup runneth over. Surely goodness and mercy shall follow me all the days of my life: and I will dwell in the house of the Lord forever.

Psalm 23

SOME EARLY CONCLUSIONS

Men explore, invent, discover, innovate, and produce great works; but regardless of whether they are men of faith or not, it is God Who inspires them, gives them insight and makes them fruitful. However, we will not understand all mysteries while in this life. We need to accept God's mysteries, some will become resolved as we mature, others will not. We must remember that we are creatures. We may become one with God, but we will never become His equal. Our faith is simple and straightforward even though it is a lifelong learning process. As the Bible acknowledges in Isaiah 28: 10 "For precept must be upon precept, precept upon precept; line upon line, line upon line; here a little, and there a little:"

Finally, from my study of the Bible and what I believe has been my spiritual experience, I have arrived at the following conclusions— I do not claim that they are God's truth, although for me they are— at least at this point in my life. Jesus died for us, His enemies, but not in a process of killing others. He died in loving compliance with God's plan. When one dies for his friends it must be by giving up his life for truth and love but hopefully not by taking lives of others in the process. Aggressive patriotism and religion rarely justify killing. We may fight to our death for loved ones, as we are not yet fully mature Christians, even so we must try to stop short of killing.

I believe that the heart controls the emotions, the mind controls thought, and that the soul controls behavior. The soul is controlled by the spirit which may be: <u>of the self</u>, a resultant of experience and learning, and so is relative and changeable, prone to error and susceptible to Satan's influence and control; <u>of Satan</u>, who is the cause of all evil, and is temporal, and will cease to exist in our eternity; or <u>of God</u> the Holy Spirit, Who is truth, love, life, and is eternal and unchangeable. Once God touches our spirit with His Holy Spirit, the bond is permanent and gradually leads to the conversion of our spirit as one with His Spirit, and becomes immortal; this eventually becomes reflected in our soul (our behavior), if not, the bond may never have occurred.

An Important Postscript

This could be a postscript to the preceding passages. Postscripts are usually something important left out. Perhaps it is akin to someone going 'psst' in order to reveal a secret. Often a young child will say something very important just as a casual aside and if you are not listening or attending, it will be missed. The following is of such major importance and since it was only alluded to in the foregoing pages, I thought it well to expand on the matter. The following scriptural quotation was listed above but must be emphasized.

But without faith it is impossible to please Him: for he that cometh to God must believe that He is, and that He is a rewarder of them that diligently seek Him.

Hebrews 11:6

God has imparted faith to His elect-before birth. This gift is eternal and cannot be lost, God does not take back something He has given. Philippians 1:6 "Being confident of this very thing, that He which hath begun a good work in you will perform it until the day of Jesus Christ:" How or whether I use it is a different matter. The faith is two-fold, 1) that He exists, and 2) that He is a rewarder of those that **diligently seek** Him. Our 'faith' is either inoperative or non-existent **if** we believe He exists but do not **diligently seek** Him. Our faith is unfruitful if we believe He exists and we **diligently seek** Him **but** do not believe He will reward us with the fruits of the Spirit, just because we **seek** Him.

In the puzzling matter of 'election', let us go back to scripture to see what it states about this important concept. I say concept because the word itself is dependent upon our interpretation of the verses in the Bible that refer to it. To me the conclusion of the matter of election is that it means, if you want to believe-you can, if you want to be saved-you can be. This was all determined by God's foreknowledge of what were to be our eventual decisions and choices as we experience life wherein we have freedom of choice, between good and evil. God is a loving God and as Paul said in 1Timothy 2:3-4; "For this is good and acceptable in the sight of God our Saviour; Who will have **all men to be saved**, and come unto the knowledge of the truth."

Furthermore, concerning election: 1Peter 1:2 "Elect according to the foreknowledge of God the Father, through sanctification of the Spirit, unto obedience and sprinkling of the blood of Jesus Christ:.." So the indication here is that it is a process-sanctification. This is a good place to insert that everything about salvation and being 'saved' are processes done in steps and even being 'born again' is a birthing process. Our election is once for all and final and everlasting, but it is based upon God's foreknowledge of whether or not, during the course of ones lifetime, one undergoes the processes of sanctification, 'being saved' or 'born again'. For example it is not a matter of being 'saved' or obtaining salvation, multiple times or even once. But rather one is involved in an on-going process of choices covering a lifetime. Since God knows the outcome of your choices but you do not, even though your salvation is certain in God's foreknowledge, it is not in yours, so your security cannot be once and for all in your mind. Ones certainty rests on the assurance given by the Holy Spirit because we all continue to sin, which we must confess to the Holy Spirit and repent. If 'eternal security' were a human condition it would vastly reduce the necessity of the Holy Spirit's presence. (see Titus 3:4-8 and 1Corinthians 2:11). Of what need would there be of hope, if there were no doubt, if we knew our salvation was secured and eternal? Yet hope is listed right up there in importance with love and faith! Furthermore, hope is stressed throughout the New Testament. This is necessary because we continue to sin, even though less often and less grievously. Later on we will use 'eternal security' as an example of an unscriptual and counter-productive man-made doctrine that causes more doubts than it dispels.

What often happens with someone who has faith is that he confuses the matter by believing it is his faith and not God's grace that saves him. In other words God does reward us for using the faith which He has bestowed upon us to diligently seek Him and to know that He **will** reward us for this. Our goodness and loyalty are most important. But it is God's grace, His steadfastness, truth and love which insure our salvation. And so, if we have been gifted with faith, we can be secure in it **if** we **diligently seek** Him and expect Him to reward us. His Grace is eternal and therefore our destination is secure and eternal. But the degree of our feeling of security is dependent upon our walk in the Holy Spirit. Security and salvation are often confused with each other, as are feelings and reality.

GETTING SIDETRACKED

At this point we get into a more detailed study of what concluded the previous section. As an example of 'theological' dogma and post-apostolic doctrine getting in the way of Christian relationships, I am going to discuss the doctrines of Eternal Security and the doctrine of Works. This may be very upsetting for someone who interprets the Bible differently. But what is the point of arguing about it or breaking up into different denominations? That would be sad and has resulted in the sorry state of Christianity today. Bear with me as I launch into my belief about works, security, and salvation from my interpretation of the Bible. By the way, I may change these beliefs or interpretations in the future. But I do not believe that makes me a bad person or an unsaved person, in fact, it may result from an ability to grow. Being rigid is not necessarily the same thing as being faithful to the truth. Being able to grow in insight and understanding is when one acquires wisdom. The truth is eternal and unchanging and we continue to try to approach God's truth.

Not only is His faith eternal but so is His faithfulness toward those He has chosen, that is, His elect. **However**, our <u>assurance</u> (security) may not be secure because it varies with the: 1) persistence of our belief in Him; 2) constancy of seeking Him; and 3) strength of our expectation of His rewarding us (the kind or type of reward may not be known). Beyond our knowledge that it will be all the fruits of the Spirit and perhaps some of His gifts as well. Thus assurance (security) depends upon us **abiding** in Him, as Christ said in John 15:14 "**Abide** in Me, and I in you, as the branch cannot bear fruit of itself, except it **abide** in the vine; no more can ye, except ye **abide** in Me." He refers to abiding in Him in dozens of other places in the New Testament and it means living in Him. Now another key word to our understanding is the word, **'seek'**, which is used in the New Testament, for example, Matthew 6:33, "But **seek** ye first the Kingdom of God, and His righteousness; and all these things shall be added unto you." Here, 'seek' is an active verb, requiring effort on our part.

Consider the implications and meanings of the following, John 17:11, "And now I am no more in the world, but these are in the world, and I come to Thee. Holy Father, keep through thine own name those whom Thou hast given Me, that they may be **one**, as we are." If we are to be **one** with Him, think of what that means in terms of our: dedication, persistence, fruitfulness, character and life! Listen to the strength of Jesus' speech here, John 15:14, "Ye are my friends, **if** ye do whatsoever I command you." Another word fraught with meaning is 'follow', for example, John 12:26, "If any man serve Me, let him **follow** me; and where I am, there shall also My servant be: if any man serve Me, him will My Father honor." Thus, **we are to follow His way,** we are therefore to have 'works' or a 'walk'.

Doctrinairism has caused a lot of trouble, after all is not faith a gift and not earned? It certainly is! Listen again to Paul in his letter to Ephesians 2: 8-9, "For by grace are ye saved through faith; and that not of yourselves: it is the **gift** of God: **Not of works,** lest any man should **boast**." This does **not** mean to say we should not have works (Ephesians 2:10). 'For we are his workmanship created in Christ Jesus unto good works which God hath before ordained that we should walk in them.'

To my way of thinking, this means we are saved by Christ, but we must show our faith by our works. The doctrine of eternal security could mean to some that basically once you are saved you are eternally secure. What I see as the pernicious part of this doctrine is that there are those who understand this to mean that you should **always** be confident of this awareness and certainty. Otherwise there is either something wrong with your faith or you were never saved in the first place!? This is the stance of some of the adherents to this doctrine. But the Spirit is grieved if we sin (and we will) and thereupon we lose His assurance, but not our salvation!

Now here it can be particularly false and debilitating because it **denies** that ones lack of assurance is due to a lack of works and obedience to Christ and the New Testament. That would then make salvation dependent on works, these adherents say!

So then the only conclusion one can reach is: If I doubt my security, I must not be saved, because I am supposed to have eternal security (that is, be aware of it at all times)! People who defend this doctrine continually interchange salvation and security which is not warranted at all, in fact, it is a non-sequitor based on the false premise of equating salvation and security.

If you are one of the elect, that is, blest with faith, you will not lose your salvation but you may very well lose your security, if you do not have a walk of works. If one is not brought to this understanding by grieving the Spirit, feeling lost and being unfruitful (as did Lot, in the Old Testament), then perhaps that one is not one of the elect and so truly does not have salvation. If one is without works and therefore miserable, he most likely is one of the elect and still has his salvation (because it is eternal). But to say that we don't have to be obedient because that would be works and would in effect make Christ's sacrifice insufficient by itself, is false. We obey because we love Him and want to please Him and because we are influenced by the Holy Spirit. This has nothing to do with earning or deserving salvation!

Modeling after our Lord and consonant with His commands, we walk the walk-of works, and not in order to earn our salvation (which we can not) and which **is** ours already, if we are of the elect. This does not mean that we earn our salvation, but how do we know we are one of the 'elect' if we do not bear fruit as our Lord did and urged us to do. Without this how can we know we are a 'family' member? "I am the **way**, the truth, and the life: no man cometh unto the Father, but by Me." John 14:6. This means, we are to do as He did!

But many well meaning souls have lost not only their fruitfulness but their deep abiding joy and genuine assurance because some dedicated theologians innocently emphasize a misleading doctrinal interpretation of Paul's statement in his letter to the Ephesians (2:8-9) as quoted above. They over zealously push this and create out of it a man-made *doctrine* of 'Eternal Security'. God (through His foreknowledge of how our lives would culminate) has chosen those belonging to Christ long before they were born; but although they have innocently been mislead about eternal security, they are still saved!

"And we know that all things work together for good to them that love God, to them who are the **called** according to His purpose. For whom He did foreknow, He also did predestinate to be **conformed** to the image of His Son, that He might be the firstborn among many brethren. Moreover whom He did predestinate, them He also called: and whom He called, them He also justified: and whom He justified, them He also glorified." Romans 8: 28-30.

Furthermore, "Blessed be the God and Father of our Lord Jesus Christ, Who has **blessed us with all spiritual blessings** in heavenly places in Christ: According as He hath chosen us in Him before the foundation of the world, that we should be **holy and without blame in Him in love**: Having predestinated us unto the adoption of children by Jesus Christ Himself, according to the good pleasure of His will, **To the praise of the glory of His grace**, wherein He hath made us accepted in the beloved." Ephesians 1:3-6.

Now if we do not have a walk that follows Jesus with works-where are those **'blessings'** referred to and how are we **'holy without blame before Him in love:'**

and how are we showing '**the glory of His grace**'? Or how are we to be **'conformed'** to His image?

We are the elect and we had better reveal this in our lives. The devil is so clever as to even mislead the 'elect'. "For there shall arise false Christs, and false prophets, and shall shew great signs and wonders; inasmuch that, if it were possible, they shall deceive the very elect." Matthew 24:24. Furthermore, "But shun profane and vain babblings: for they will increase unto more ungodliness. And their word will eat as doth a canker: of whom is Hymenaeus and Philetus; Who concerning the truth have erred, saying that the resurrection is past already; and overthrow the faith of some." 2Timothy 2:16-18.

In John 14:14-15 Jesus said, "If ye shall ask anything in My name, I will do it. **If** ye love Me, keep My commandments." What did He mean? What could He have meant by the phrase, 'in My name'? If one is asking in someone's name, is not he revealing himself as representing that person? If so, wouldn't that mean or imply that he held the same values and character as the person for whom he was asking?

Jesus said He would give anything asked for, but here again the way it is put, 'in His name' would not that mean that one would be asking for things of which He would approve? Who would assume that therefore one would ask for a Cadillac, a million dollars, or for someone to be cursed-as a few examples? No, the fruits of the Spirit are: love, joy, peace, patience, gentleness, goodness, faith, temperance, and humility. The gifts of the Spirit are: teaching, prophesying, healing, ministry, wisdom, miracles, and faith, to name some of them.

Christ came not only to save us but to show us how we were to be! There are plenty of instances where He said, in effect, if you do not obey Me-you are none of Mine. He also said that if one does not love others, one is not of God! What do things like that mean? Certainly not that we will lose our salvation but rather He is saying that such a person is possibly not of the 'elect'! We cannot afford to be made into lazy Christians by some carelessly used doctrine such as 'eternal security'. If we are, we will surely lose our rewards here and perhaps hereafter.

Once the Holy Spirit has sealed us we are saved for all eternity. If we walk after Christ and do as He asked us to do, then we can know that the Holy Spirit has bonded with our spirit, and our life will change. And as long as we walk after the Holy Spirit we can and will have assurance and security. Another result of the Christian life that Jesus referred to in John 5:29, "And shall come forth (from the graves); they that have done good, unto the resurrection of life; and they that have done evil, unto the resurrection of damnation." Thus the doctrine of eternal security minimizes the work of the Holy Spirit.

Security varies with the closeness of our walk with the Holy Spirit. The elect have eternal salvation. One can have an almost constant and growing sense of being one of the elect of God who were given to Christ but not by resting on his laurels and beginning to relegate the Holy Spirit to something less than an almost constant presence. To do this would almost certainly introduce a question of our election.

We need to continue to look to and call upon the Spirit because the 'old nature' or animal part of us dies slowly and Satan lurks behind every shadow. Listen to Paul in his letter to the Romans Chapter 7 verses 15-18. "For that which I do I allow not: for what I would, that do I not; but what I hate, that do I. If then I do that which I would not, I consent unto the law that it is good. Now then it is no more I that do it, but sin that dwelleth in me. For I know that in me (that is, in my flesh,) dwelleth no good thing: for to will is present with me; but how to perform that which is good I find not." In the next chapter he goes on to say, "There is therefore now no condemnation to them which are in Christ Jesus, who walk not after the flesh, but after the Spirit." Romans 8:1. We must continually rely on the Holy Spirit for guidance and help. The dogma of 'eternal security' is counterproductive and could encourage some to grieve the Spirit without qualms. Of incomparably more value is the comfort and sanctifying work of the Holy Spirit.

If a person is by and large a 'good' person and has had no baffling tragedies or corrupting influences in his life he is apt to feel that he is acceptable to God without accepting Christ and walking after the Spirit. This is both a snare and a illusion and if this remains his belief, then such a person is eternally lost. But the problem of hibernating sin is always present and evil is just waiting for the opportunity to take over and engulf a person. This is an always present possibility because every human who has not been 'born again' has the potential of committing the grossest, most monstrous sins and thereby to be and do evil. All one has to do is to scratch the skin of our world or even to do some earnest soul searching, if there is any lingering doubt as to the truth of this reality. This realization can stir up a mixture of melancholy and anger! Somewhere within can be found an engulfing comprehension of what evil man has produced amid such opportunity!

One of the most evocative passages in all of literature is contained in Paul's letter to the Romans, verses 7:14 through 8:14.

These lines portray the heart of the human condition, its problem, and its solution.

Its profundity and simplicity have the exquisitness of truth.

It is highly recommended that these verses be read and reread in your bible at your own leisure.

Why are there troubles, heartbreak, commercial failures, death, illness, accidents, loss and so much hurt and tragedy? Maybe in part this is due to the possibility that humans (or most of them) would never seek God, much less want and need faith, without these sorrows and difficulties.

SOME PERSONAL INTERPRETATIONS

I have never heard of the existence of cold fire, if fire had no warmth it would be useless for the maintenance of life. It is possible to be in the presence of fire and not feel its warmth such as when one is too far away from a campfire on a winter's night. The sun despite the intensity and magnitude of its fire and heat, passes its rays through space without warming it. However, when its rays strike certain objects or mediums they resonate with warmth from the sun. There can be light without fire and without warmth as there can be warmth without fire but there cannot be fire without producing heat.

There cannot be eternal life without God. God is love. There is no love without God and thus there cannot be eternal life without love. Humans are made to resonate God's love and when they fulfill this function they have eternal life. Man cannot do this without God and God grants His love only to those in Jesus Christ. That is, those who accept Jesus Christ as His Son, acknowledge their need of Him and live according to the Holy Spirit. In fact, this acceptance or rejection of Jesus Christ is the only act of free will a human has because when he decides to accept Jesus Christ then

God (through His foreknowledge) grants this and follows through with His gift of faith in His Son and the presence of His Holy Spirit, in accordance with the New Testament of the Holy Bible. Thereafter and in all other actions or decisions man has only freedom of choice. If he never makes this one act of free will then his entire life is made up only of choices. He chooses whether to follow the impulses of Satan or the 'Self.'

So Man is a 'receptor' of impulses from God or from Satan and 'Self', and if of the former then he becomes a 'resonator' of God's love. It is from this that a human 'knows' (at times it is just a hope) that he will have eternal life. That is, whether or not he feels God's love (at first it is a faint and subtle feeling, but grows stronger as the Christian matures) and transmits it to those around him.

In these perilous times it is vital to remember that our first allegiance spiritually is to God and that our first duty, emotionally and physically is to our family. As far as our country goes we are to obey its laws and its rulers in all instances except in cases that would violate Christ and His commands. Because Christ, the Apostles, and Paul set forth our road map and our charter, it is necessary that we study the New Testament rigorously. We must learn to make our lives conform to

His commandments and their teachings in thought and behavior, in mind and in heart.

This is not easy because we have our old human nature to cope with which has resulted from our genes, experiences and the spiritual realm and I quote; "For we wrestle not against flesh and blood, but against principalities, against powers, against the rulers of the darkness of this world, against spiritual wickedness in high places."(Ephesians 6:12).

Our purpose is to grow from being essentially an animal (carnal) to becoming Spiritual beings. "For they that are after the flesh do mind the things of the flesh; but they that are after the Spirit the things of the Spirit. For to be carnally minded is death; but to be spiritually minded is life and peace. Because the carnal mind is enmity against God: for it is not subject to the law of God, neither indeed can be. So then they that are in the flesh cannot please God." (Romans 8:5-8)

The individual Christian is part of a corporate body called the Church. Remember this is capitalized and does not mean any church or denomination on earth but rather it is the body of Christ who is the head. It is in this sense that the individual must deny 'self' because the Church is everything, and in denying ones 'self' we become one with Christ and are part of His body, the Church. The Church must go on, must survive and will survive and eventually will glorify God. When we die our spirit goes directly to be with the Lord. When He returns for the 'rapture' of the Church, we will receive our 'glorified bodies' "For the Lord Himself shall descend from heaven with a shout, with the voice of the archangel, and with the trump of God: and the dead in Christ shall rise first: Then we which are alive and remain shall be caught up together with them in the clouds, to meet the Lord in the air: and so shall we ever be with the Lord." (1 Thessalonians 4:16-17).

This is known as the 'rapture' of the Church. "In a moment, in the twinkling of an eye, at the last trump: for the trumpet shall sound, and the dead shall be raised incorruptible, and we shall be changed."(1Corinthians 15:52). So those who have already died will receive their 'glorified' bodies first and then those who are still alive will go to meet the Lord (with their spirit) and then they will receive their 'glorified' or incorruptible bodies. This will be in the end times. At that time Christ draws all the 'saints' ('born again' ones or the 'saved' ones) up to Him in the air.

After seven years of tribulation on earth, wherein more people are 'saved' especially numerous will be the Jewish people (according to my understanding). Then will come the battle of Armageddon and Christ shall defeat all the forces (and people) of evil and shall rule for a thousand years, with the resurrected saints. After this Satan will be loosed for a while then Christ will throw him and all evil or damned souls into the everlasting fire. After that will come a new heaven and a new earth where the 'saved' will live forever in paradise.(Revelation 20:4-21:8).

If we are Christians our struggle ends with the 'Rapture'. Thus all the terrors and torments of those days will be reserved for those yet living but still 'unsaved'. Some will accept Christ during the 'Tribulation', others will continue to reject God and ultimately be damned.

Back to the present, we cannot be an army of Christian soldiers actually fighting for the Church because the Church is not a human organization with buildings. It is not an organization. It is a Spiritual body. As pointed out before, there are formal human churches with their sects, denominations and divisions. Some of which are good and useful, all of which, most likely, contain some real Christians. These human churches have been essential in handing down the Word of God, the Bible, and in maintaining some semblance of worship to the one and only God. There have been many religious wars by or between the churches and this is a sad fact. If we are to die it should be as martyrs for the Lord, passively not aggressively. For Christians, 'Holy

War' is an oxymoron (a contradiction). Our warfare is against Satan and our carnal minds.

Yes, every day we must start over again. We still have our old human nature. Just because we understand and accept the Bible as 'The Truth' does not mean we can rest on our laurels. We are in a world that we are not to be 'of'. Which means that we have to contend every day with the 'world, the flesh, and the devil'. Or putting it another way, we have a daily struggle against giving in to 'the lust of the eyes, the lust of the flesh, and the pride of life'. On top of all this we must cope with death, loss, disease, and other tragic, hurtful events.

As we study the Bible and strive to put it into practice we often find that it is open to different interpretations, I think, intentionally so, because God demands faith. Time and again both in life and in the Bible our faith is called upon. Our God is a God of **love** who gives us faith which often requires hope. We must love others, good and bad, friends and enemies. Our 'love' may vary from family love, to best friends to acquaintances whom we like, to people that reject or dislike us and even hurt us (in these cases it would perhaps be more accurate to say, at most, we accept them when we can but, at worst, we do not hate them. Hate is a cancer that can consume its possessor).

Christ's work is done, He has defeated sin, death, and Satan. All that is to be done by Christians is to accept Christ as the Son of God and our Savior and to deny our 'selves', follow Christ-His way, His life and His truth. Christ's work is completed, we cannot undo it nor can we add to it, it is finished for all eternity. Our faith is shown in and by our lives. To the extent that we live in love toward all, reveals the degree that faith is active in us. Without faith in Christ we cannot please God, nor can we be saved!

At first, most of us live more in hope than in faith but then as faith is nurtured and drawn on we have more faith and fall back on hope less, but are never completely free of the need of hope in our lives. Through the help of the Holy Spirit we become more loving and are increasingly blessed with all the fruits of the Spirit and some of His gifts.

Some Personal Interpretations

PART 3

SCIENCE, ART, AND FAITH

Science is based upon information from the senses. It also infers a thing's existence from the feedback from something else, for example, the 'existence' of an atom from the movement of particles in a cloud chamber. Art activates the senses by manipulation of things to arouse emotion. Faith controls the senses and the emotions by revelation, logic, imagination, and experience. When men through their senses and/ or their emotions try to prove the negative about faith through these means, they are no longer in neither the realm of science nor art. Faith is a gift and results in profound changes within the human being. Both science and art make use of 'faith' in their endeavors, that is, utilizing belief in certain physical procedures that will hopefully result in certain material, physical, spatial, sensual, or emotional results. For example, when Edison experimented on finding a filament to use in the electric light bulb, or when Degas utilized certain colors and painting techniques to express what he saw.

Freud and Darwin were scientists who both ranged beyond their borders and made unwarranted statements on matters of faith which neither could confirm nor disprove. Despite all their great scientific findings they were still men and displayed their shortcomings and fallacies in these extensions beyond their realms of capabilities. Some of Freud's statements will be held up as examples of a scientist's impotence, when he makes unwarranted and unproved statements about 'laws' of life or of the universe.

The following were excerpted from Freud's, "Civilization and Its Discontents". (Great Books of the Western World; Robert Hutchins, Editor in Chief, Volume 54-Freud; William Benton, Publisher; Encyclopedia Brittanica,1952.)

"In my *Future of an Illusion* I was concerned much less with the deepest sources of religious feeling than with what the ordinary man understands by his religion, that system of doctrines and pledges that on the one hand explains the riddle of this world to him with an enviable completeness, [underlining is mine] and on the other assures him that a solicitous Providence is watching over him and will make it up to him in a future existence for any short-comings in this life. The ordinary man cannot imagine this Providence in any other form but that of a greatly exalted father, for only such a one could understand the needs of the sons of men, or be softened by their prayers and placated by the signs of their remorse. The whole thing is so patently infantile, so incongruous with reality, that to one whose attitude to humanity is friendly it is painful to think that the great majority of mortals will never be able to rise above this view of life..." (page 771).

"...the tendency to aggression is an innate independent, instinctual disposition in man, and I come back now to the statement that it constitutes the most powerful obstacle to culture. At one point in this discussion, the idea took possession of us that culture was a peculiar process passing over human life and we are still under the influence of this idea. We may add to this that the process proves to be in the service of Eros, which aims at binding together single human individuals, then families, then tribes, races, nations, into one great unity, that of humanity. Why this has to be done we do not know; it is simply the work of Eros. [underlining is mine] These masses of men must be bound to one another libidinally; necessity alone, the advantages of common work, would not hold them together. The natural instinct of aggressiveness in man, the hostility of each one against all and of all against each one, opposes this program of civilization. This instinct of aggression is the derivative and main representative of the death instinct we have found alongside Eros, sharing his rule over the earth. And now, it seems to me, the meaning of the evolution of culture is no longer a riddle to us. [underlining is mine]. It must present to us the struggle between Eros and death, between the instincts of life and the instincts of destruction, as it works itself out in the human species. This struggle is what all life essentially consists of [underlining is mine] and so the evolution of civilization may be simply described as the struggle of the human species for existence. And it is this battle of the Titans that our nurses and governesses try to compose with their lullaby-song of heaven." (page 791)

In the first quote above he accuses anyone with faith as "...explaining the world with enviable completeness...", see the parts underlined. Then in the second quote he states, "... is no longer a riddle to us..." referring to the, "meaning of the evolution of culture..." He also states what the struggle of all life, "...essentially consists of..." See the underlined passages. He talks about having all the answers to culture, life and death, and boxing them up and tying a bow ribbon around it! He accuses religion as being guilty of exactly that of which he is guilty!

There is this unexplained derision of religion by certain otherwise intelligent men, sometimes even geniuses. **What unmitigated arrogance!** It is one thing to be angry at the crimes committed in the name of religion, but that is what religion sometimes becomes, a faith corrupted by men's greed and lust for power. But some scientists who, of all people, slander faith because of what some leaders, who were followers of the initiators of the faith, did is an exhibition of very prejudicial thinking. One more quote from Freud, "Once the apostle Paul had laid down universal love between all men as the foundation of his Christian community, the inevitable consequence in Christianity was the utmost intolerance towards all who remained outside of it..." (page 788) What an over generalization and ignoring of the faith itself and its initial adherents, as well as many of the common people who constituted its membership over the ages.

When one really thinks about this stance that both Darwin and Freud took regarding the fundamental Christian faith, its tenets, founders, and demonstrations; it is more than appalling-it has the taint of Satan's subtlety, deceit and destructiveness about it. Satan the 'great' manipulator and deceiver has similarly worked among many college professors and some theologians who have been carried away by erroneous thinking. Many in these last two groups were merely pawns of the devil, some of whom were mislead innocently; others because their minds were seduced by conceit or blinded by ambition-with no underlying intent to deceive or harm. I do not use Satan and the devil lightly, however unintentional these errors were they have done much harm by causing many young people to falter in their faith and be thrown into a maize of confusion or aimlessness! Over the centuries there were no doubt some few theologians and many church leaders who were motivated by the lust for power and control.

Freud and Darwin cannot account for a handful of simple, uneducated, frightened men suddenly becoming heroic in facing all odds, after the resurrection of Christ. No figment of the imagination can account for this and the fact that the faith has continued for thousands of years. The Bible does not whitewash its main characters. (look at David and Bathsheeba, Noah, Jacob, etc.). Already most of the prophesies of the Old Testament have been fulfilled in Christ and the few remaining prophesies give all the signs of being about to be fulfilled in the current history of Israel. Prophesies have been made by dozens of men over centuries of time, yet all agreeing. The Bible is made up of 66 books, spanning 4500 years, written by 50 some men, and yet is consistent in its doctrines. Its validity does not rest upon only the actual miracles performed throughout its pages!

Science and art need to leave faith in a realm of its own; it operates on different truths and principles.

Many artists have contributed to the worship and awe of God the Creator over the centuries. Interestingly, now that we are in an age of such 'miraculous' scientific discoveries, the ranks of scientists are increasing who concede that there is a Creator and some give credence to the Christian version. And ironically enough, there seems to be a larger number of artists who today, when peace and prosperity are more prevalent, express doubt and/or derision in their works, about God and faith?!

Faith is a gift from God and it is given by God through His foreknowledge. At this point in our understanding this represents a mystery as far beyond us as that of the Trinity and the existence of evil. There seems to be little doubt that if one wants faith, it is available, but it must be accepted and lived by.

WONDER AND AWE

The wonder and awe of God Almighty, where is it? The ancient Jews (Israelites) would not even write His name much less say it! If we have any wonder or awe it is toward Man and his accomplishments. Our buildings, rocket ships, television, skyscrapers, medical discoveries, great metropolitan complexes, and even athletic stars and business tycoons and figures of history, draw forth some awe toward men. Yet we are merely creatures and every accomplishment of ours has been inspired by the God Who created our complex, miraculous brain.

Adam and Eve hid from God in the Garden of Eden; but how and where can we hide? Is our lack of wonder going to become an eternity of terror and hell when our final day comes before His judgment seat? Does the ferocity of tornadoes, hurricanes, lightning, floods and earthquakes frighten us? Can we even be terrorized by nightmares or panic attacks, or crazy (insane) people? Some of us walk around in a trance of unfeelingness, unappreciation, non-worship. There will not be any feeling when our bodies lie dead in the grave, in fact, that might be the fondest hope of some, that when this life is over it is all over. But all will stand before **Him** for a cursing or blessing.

If any person stops and considers what God has given us, how He has protected us, never totally letting go of us; and He has been so unendingly patient and loving with us-all things considered. When every command He has given us has been for our own well-being. If simply by accepting His Son and trying to obey His commandments and following His way of life will bring us eternal bliss, why is it we still look for rewards in Heaven? Will not it be enough to be in His presence where there will be no tears, pain, loss, or hurt but quite the contrary, love, joy, peace, faith, etc. Does not it seem natural for us to try to please Him while we are here, to strive to be good sons and daughters, especially since He is willing to forgive our every sin as well as our miserable past?

Can we doubt that evil forces of darkness confuse and cause such intelligent creatures as we not to love our Father Creator, and obey His commands? It is time already for us to seek to please Him and to have some awe and worship for Him. This should not be done by rote or mechanically and without putting our full selves into it. Does the thought of all this seem exhausting? We need help, His help. We need only to try and to acknowledge that Jesus is the Son of God Who shed

His blood for us and rose from the dead. And upon our asking He will send the Holy Spirit to help us change. He will give us Love, Joy and Peace, here and now, wherever we live, what ever we do. Gradually our life takes on meaning and we find it possible to love others and get rid of negative thoughts and self-hate.

If one has a tyrannical boss or an abusive spouse it is possible to live with him or her. After all, Daniel survived the Lions den, Moses took the children of Israel through the midst of the sea, the Apostles healed people and even brought them back from death. Let us not feel the necessity of making this an apologetic for faith! Faith is faith in the 'unbelievable'; so let us apply it to our own lives, reverently, intelligently, consistently, and persistently. Those early martyrs who did not live long enough to ever leave the Roman coliseums, soared out of there in their spirits to be with Jesus. Which is what we will do the instant we die; we will not even approach the grave, we will be long gone.

If someone has ruined our life through drugs or deceit we can be happy again, strong and victorious in our precious Lord. Nothing can ever destroy us and even life in this terrible world will take on a positive complexion that defeats depression, anxiety, and illness. (One's spirit will be long gone but one's body will have to await the rapture).

This is a terrible world, far beyond what many of us experience. But God is love, truth, life, and beauty; and He will never, never let us go or perish if we will turn to Him and keep turning to Him, even when it seems hopeless or even if and when it becomes a matter of returning to Him. He will forgive our failures and mistakes; He will make it possible for us to hang in there. He has told us that Satan corrupted the world and brought any and all evil into it. Let us place the blame, where it belongs-in the devil's lap. Merely because we are creatures neither means that we are dumb nor without understanding; but it does mean that we are not the Creator and His ways are often beyond our understanding. But because He is a God of love, make no mistake about that (which is exactly what Satan wants us to do), He does all things well and someday we will know the answers, as He has promised. (1 Corinthians 13: 12).

We must never forget that God is love and we are His love children and are precious to Him-we must not let anyone dissuade us from this certainty. He is the Rock, and we are part of Him, grains of His granite. We are here to glorify Him and when we do we live partly in His glory in this life; and what is ahead for us in Heaven is beyond words to describe. Our traitorous mind will become spiritual and be one with the Holy Spirit; our decrepit or degenerating body will become a new and glorified body, capable of changing back and forth from physical to spiritual with abilities undreamed of. (See John 20: 24-28) The Kingdom of God will be undefinable, indescribable, eternal Paradise where everybody loves everybody.

Our purpose on earth is to glorify God and live a life of love. Eventually evil will be defeated and disappear for ever. There will be no competition, envy, striving, or status; it will be Heaven. We will become that perfect Man and Woman of God's first creation having metamorphosed from very good to perfect-and wonder of wonders, God will have let us have had a hand in it! Paul the Apostle said we should be in constant prayer. It is reasonable to arrive at the conclusion that just to think about God, even with vague thoughts (even unworded) of thanksgiving and praise, is prayer. It might be helpful to fill in the rest of this page with praise and worship directed to God. It is a start. Just keep holding on to that thread of praise and worship as you think of it and before long you will have a whole cloth of many colors to spread before the Lord.

Remember, one of God's blessings may be loss, illness, or tragedy, if that is what activates one's faith in Christ Jesus.

KEEP ON GOING

Finally, it is decision time if you want to have more faith; just think this prayer.

Jesus, I want you to be Lord of my life. I am a sinner. I cannot undo what I have done, nor can I stop sinning to any consistent, satisfactory degree. I need your help, please send the Holy Spirit to me, to lead me, guide me, comfort me and strengthen me. Receive my confessions daily and help me to repent.

The Son of God died for us and sends us God's Holy Spirit to make us new persons. This is your 'conception' and you are now in the birthing process of becoming one with Him, forever. Joy, peace, love, and faith will be yours, each day a little more.

We need to overcome the fear of failing now and then. We need to ask forgiveness and help in not repeating that backsliding but rather continuing to grow into Christian maturity, day by day.

"For it is by grace you have been saved, through faith-and this not from yourselves, it is the gift of God-not by works, so that no one can boast. For we are God's workmanship, created in Christ Jesus to do good works, which God prepared in advance

for us to do." (Ephesians 2:8-10) New International Version. [underlining is mine].

Our security depends upon our walk but our salvation does not depend upon our security.

The Christian, even more than the physician, 'shall do no harm!' The Christian is also to be loving in his relationships.

ABOUT THE AUTHOR

The author is a clinical psychologist in private practice giving psychotherapy to individuals, families, and couples for over twenty-five years. He was chief psychologist in the heroin program for the city of Detroit for five years. He was an executive general manager of a furniture factory for twelve years. He also volunteered for the naval air force, serving four years active duty as a commissioned officer.